Auntie   Erin's

A B C

Book
of

African
Animals

Auntie Erin's
A B C
Book
of
African
Animals

Summary: An ABC book of African animal photography with informative text.

ISBN: 979-8-218-0626

For Carl (Editor-in-Chief), Alex and Erin, whose brilliant minds, exceptional wit, and loving hearts were an inspiration for this book.

Antelopes stop to eat and drink.
They love to run and leap I think.
If they see anyone off they'll go!
Impossible to follow!

Baboons are dangerous
and attracted by food

Busy **b**a**b**oons gra**bb**ing **b**ugs
Regarding me suspiciously.
If I had **b**rought a **b**ag of **b**uns
They might **b**e gra**bb**ing me!

Cunningly ra**c**es the **c**heetah.
All **c**reatures it **c**an beat.
Its pa**c**e is fast but **c**annot last
For it **c**ould overheat!

A **d**eer it appears **d**reaming in **di**sguise
With ears as big as bats.
I never thought I'**d** ever see
Deer with ears like that!

Ee

Enormous elephant enjoying a puddle
Stomping feet eager to cuddle.
Enthusiastically entreats me to play
By emitting with its trunk a spray!

"Fraaaahhnk!"
Fluffed feathered heron sings.
"GO! GO! GO!" for fearful sightings.
Graceful flight lofty height.
Magnificent powerful wings.

Gg

Good **g**rief! Don't lau**g**h at **g**iraffes.
They may **g**reet you with scorn.
For after an acacia meal
They spit out twi**g**s and thorns!

How do **h**ippos stay afloat?
So **h**uge. So **h**eavy. So **h**ippopotumussy.
"So w**h**at?" **t**hey say
And float away.

Ii

Insects here insects there.
Insects insects everywhere.
Under a net is one's best bet
For inhaling bugless air!

Jovial jagged warthog
Jumping in the bog.
With jumbo jaws and jutting claws
Jousting near a log.

Kori Bustard have you heard
Is a **k**ind of aw**k**ward **k**ing of birds.
Known not for beauty or its wings
But as the heaviest of flying things!

Lazy lions look at me.
I wonder what they see?
Lunch .... or company?

Mm

Monkeys don't like water much.
It has to them an unmonkey touch.
On a boat they'd rather float
With yummy grapes to clutch.

Nn
Nests on
splendid branches
nodding.
Havens
far from human
prodding.

Oo

Lovely le**o**pard eyeing me
Thr**o**ugh a turf **o**f tangled twigs.
Thinks I cann**o**t see h**o**w beautiful it is.

Perched speckled pigeon
Chirps a persuasive "DOO! DOO!
Yapping happily.

Qq

Quietly stalks the spotted hyena
Africa's largest common carnivore.
Quirky giggly often **q**uibbly
With a heart-size **q**uite bigger by far!

Rr

Rhinoceros tries to hide from me
Searching for some privacy.
Quite a commendable effort to blend
But for the bulge at either end.

Ss

Savanna buffalo
Seek savory grass and leaves.
Without this grub will eat a shrub
Somewhat reluctantly.

Tortoise traveling to a trunk
Tiptoes through turf and thicket.
Ingesting hay along the way
And occasionally a cricket!

A k**u**d**u** in distress will catap**u**lt a fence.
J**u**mp from standing
A perfect landing!
A k**u**d**u** could. Could yo**u**?

Vv

Vervet monkey views from trees
A vista of leaves and fruits and seeds.
Often climbs down to venture to town
For alternative varieties.

Wildebeests on an afternoon journey
Wondering which path to take.
One turns to me inquisitively
"Which journey would you make?"

Xx

Rock hyra**x** on a mountaintop
Rela**x**ing on a wall.
Ne**x**t relative to the elephant
Most common e**x**tra-small!

South African Yellow-billed Hornbill
Yearning for its friend
Has yet to complain
It was assigned a name
That seems to never end.

A zebra's stripes are black and white
In formal clothing clad.
But if I had a choice for it
I'd zip it up in plaid.

www.ingramcontent.com/pod-product-compliance
Lightning Source LLC
Chambersburg PA
CBHW041629110726
48005CB00002B/551